The ultimate guide How to learn with and retain knowledge permanently. Improve your learning performance with Active Recall.

Matthew Maverick

Copyright © 2023 Matthew Maverick

Alle Rechte vorbehalten.

ISBN:

Dedication

I dedicate this book to my family who gave me time and believed in my vision. I love you.

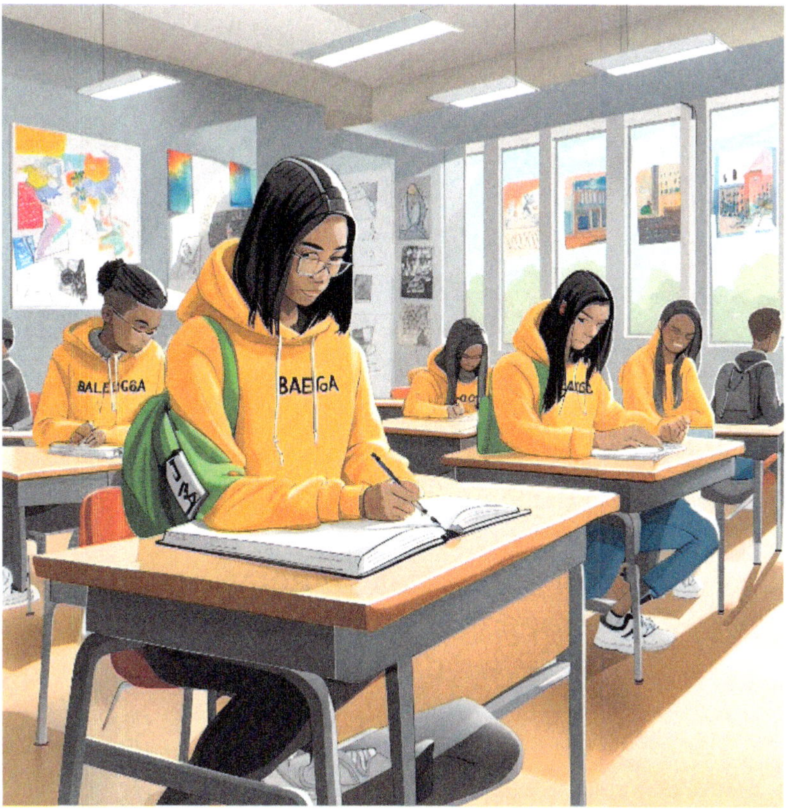

Table of Contents

- **Introduction**
  - What is Active Recall and How Does it Differ from Other Learning Methods? (Page 8)
- **Chapter 1: Understanding Active Recall**
  - Active Recall: The Ultimate Trick to Optimize Your Learning and Retain Knowledge Permanently (Page 11)
  - Discover the Secrets of Successful Students: How Active Recall Improves Your Performance (Page 15)
- **Chapter 2: Implementing Active Recall**
  - How to use Active Recall in various subjects (From the perspective of a first-year medical student) (Page 17)
  - 5 Tips for using Active Recall in preparing for and reviewing lectures and seminars (Page 18)
  - 5 Tips for incorporating Active Recall into your learning environment (Deep Work) (Page 19)
  - How can I set up my work environment to work effectively? (Page 23)
  - The power of flashcards in learning with Active Recall: How to improve your exam results and embed knowledge deeper in memory (Page 27)

- Maximize your learning performance: With these 5 tips, you create effective flashcards (Page 29)
- Maximize your exam success with summaries and Active Recall (Page 31)
- Learning Anatomy with Active Recall: A Practical Guide for Medical Students (Page 36)
- **Chapter 3: Leveraging Active Recall with Learning Techniques**
- Learning 2.0: How the Leitner System and Active Recall Lead Students to Success (Page 37)
- A Step-by-Step Guide: How to Use the Leitner System as a Student with Active Recall (Page 39)
- Maximize your exam success with the powerful testing effect (Page 39)
- Effective Learning in Legal Studies: The Testing Effect and Active Recall in Practice (Page 40)
- **Chapter 4: Enhancing Learning Efficiency**
- Maximizing Learning through Active Recall: How to Efficiently Manage Time and Energy (Page 43)
- Tips for Efficient Time and Energy Management while Practicing Active Recall Learning (Page 44)

- Maximize Your Learning Potential: How Spaced Repetition and Active Recall Collaborate to Optimize Your Memory (Page 44)
- Stress-Free Learning: The Key to Sustainable Learning Success with Active Recall (Page 45)
- 3 Tips for Adjusting Time Intervals in Learning (Page 46)
- **Chapter 5: Collaborative Learning and Goal Setting**
- Harnessing the Power of Study Groups: 3 Tips for Applying Active Recall (Page 47)
- The SMART Method: The Key to Consistent Excellence as a Student (Page 49)
- Successful Studying with SMART Goals: A Guide for (Medical) Students (Page 51)
- **Chapter 6: Overcoming Challenges**
- Challenges and Solutions in Learning through Active Recall and How to Deal with Them (Page 52)
- 3 Mistakes a (Medical) Student Could Make While Learning Active Recall and How to Avoid Them (Page 56)
- Active Recall for Students - A Summary (Page 60)
- **Bibliography (Page 64)**

Acknowledgments

I would like to thank all the students and pupils that I have mentored over the years who have inspired me to write this book. Your contributions are greatly appreciated.

Dear readers, In this book, I have primarily focused on the use of Active Recall for students from various fields of study. However, the techniques and strategies described in this book can also be applied to other areas of learning. I hope that this book is helpful for anyone interested in the topic of Active Recall and that it serves as a support in improving your learning methods and techniques.

Best of luck in reading and implementing Active Recall!

Sincerely, Matthew Maverick

What is Active Recall and How Does it Differ from Other Learning Methods?

Active Recall is a learning method in which one actively remembers information rather than just reading or listening to it. This can be a very effective method for learning and retaining information.
One way to use Active Recall is through the use of flashcards. Write the information you want to learn on a card and then ask yourself questions to recall the information. For example, if you want to remember the capital of a country, you could write on a flashcard "What is the capital of France?" and then try to recall the answer from memory.

Active Recall differs from other learning methods by actively recalling the information rather than simply regurgitating or repeating it. This can help the information to be better retained and easily retrieved. Another benefit of Active Recall is that it promotes concentration and can help in focusing on the learned material. By actively retrieving information, you have to actually engage with the material and understand it, rather than just reading or listening to it.

It's important to note that Active Recall is not the only effective learning method and that different methods work best for different people. However, it is worth considering Active Recall as an option, especially if you have difficulty remembering or focusing on what you have learned.

In this book, you will learn how to effectively use the learning method of Active Recall to improve your memory performance and exam results. You will learn how to actively recall and review your knowledge to retain it longer and how to apply the technique to optimize your study time and accelerate your learning curve. With my ultimate guide, you will learn how to tap into your full learning potential and retain your knowledge permanently. Start your journey to become a successful student now!

Active Recall: The Ultimate Trick to Optimize Your Learning and Retain Knowledge Permanently

The concept of Active Recall has become increasingly popular in recent years, particularly among students who want to optimize their learning and acquire knowledge long-term. But what exactly happens in the brain during Active Recall and what positive effects does it have?

First and foremost, it is important to understand how our brain stores and retrieves information. Typically, we learn something by hearing or reading it once and then relying on our brain to store the information for us. However, this passive learning leads to quickly forgetting what we've learned because our brain hasn't processed it actively enough.

With Active Recall, we are actively prompted to recall what we've learned by answering multiple-choice questions or using flashcards. This active process of remembering leads to our brain processing the information more thoroughly and therefore storing it better.

There are numerous studies that demonstrate the positive effects of Active Recall. A study by the University of Konstanz, for example, showed that students who prepared for an exam with Active Recall scored, on average, 50% better than students who prepared in a traditional way.

Another study by the University of Freiburg showed that Active Recall can also contribute to slowing down the forgetting of what has been learned. Students who regularly engaged in Active Recall retained knowledge longer than students who prepared passively.

As a student, there are many good reasons to familiarize yourself with the concept of Active Recall. It can improve your exam results and make your knowledge more sustainable.

Active Recall is a special learning method in which one actively retrieves and deals with what has been learned, instead of just passively absorbing and reproducing it. This type of learning has many positive effects, which have been shown in various studies.

One of the greatest advantages of Active Recall is that it helps us to understand and remember what we've learned better. When we actively engage with what we're learning and retrieve it ourselves, it is ingrained deeper into our memory and is thus easier to recall. So, it not only ensures a short-term but also long-term retention of knowledge.

Furthermore, Active Recall helps to uncover and close gaps in knowledge. When we engage with what we know and what we still don't understand during the learning process, we can work on these weak points specifically.

All in all, Active Recall is a highly effective learning technique for students who want to optimize their learning and acquire knowledge long-term. By actively engaging with the material and retrieving it ourselves, we can ensure that it is ingrained deeper into our memory and is thus easier to recall.

Discover the Secrets of Successful Students: How Active Recall Improves Your Performance

It's time to get specific. Let's put ourselves in the POINT OF VIEW (POV) of a physics student and think about how they can use the learning method of Active Recall to their advantage.

As a physics student, there are many complex concepts and equations that need to be remembered. Active Recall is a method that can help understand and retain this information better. To use Active Recall effectively, ask yourself questions about the topics you want to learn and try to recall the answers from memory.

By actively thinking about what you've learned, you can process the information better and anchor it deeper in your memory. One way to apply Active Recall in your physics studies is by recalling equations. Ask yourself questions like "What equation describes the motion of an object taking into account acceleration, velocity, and time?" and try to recall the equation from memory. This way you can better understand and apply the equations. Another way to use Active Recall is by recalling concepts. Ask yourself questions like "What is the difference between kinetic and potential energy?" and try to recall the answer from memory. By actively thinking about the concepts, you can better understand and apply them. Recalling connections is also a good way to use Active Recall in your physics studies. Ask yourself questions like "How are velocity, mass, and energy of an object related?" and try to recall the answer from memory. By actively thinking about the connections, you can better understand and apply them. It is important to note that Active Recall is not the only effective learning method and it is worth combining different techniques to process and retain what you have learned.

How to use Active Recall in various subjects (From the perspective of a first-year medical student)

Remembering Anatomy: By actively recalling the anatomy of the human body by asking oneself questions and trying to retrieve the answers from memory, one can better understand and apply anatomy. For example: "Where is the spleen located in the human body?"

Remembering Diseases and Symptoms: By actively recalling diseases and their symptoms by asking oneself questions and trying to retrieve the answers from memory, one can better understand and recognize them. For example: "What are the typical symptoms of influenza infection?"

Remembering Medicines and their Effects: By actively recalling medicines and their effects by asking oneself questions and trying to retrieve the answers from memory, one can better understand and apply them. For example: "What effect does aspirin have on the human body?"

5 Tips for using Active Recall in preparing for and reviewing lectures and seminars

Ask yourself questions: Ask yourself questions during lectures and seminars to better understand and consolidate what you have learned. For example, "What equation describes the motion of an object considering acceleration, velocity, and time?"
Create a list of important concepts and equations: After each lecture or seminar, create a list of important concepts and equations that you have learned and try to recall them from memory.
Use visual aids: Use visual aids such as diagrams, tables, and maps to better understand and retain what you have learned. For example, create a table with the names of planets and their diameters to remind yourself of the size ratios.

Create practice questions: Create practice questions about what you have learned and try to answer them from memory. For example, "What equation describes the motion of an object considering acceleration, velocity, and time?"

Use study groups: Use study groups to discuss what you have learned with others and ask each other questions to better understand and retain the material.

Preparation for German literature students

Create a list of important literary periods and their characteristic features: After each lecture or seminar, create a list of important literary periods and their characteristic features that you have learned and try to recall them from memory.
Use visual aids: Use visual aids such as timelines or mind maps to better understand and retain what you have learned. For example, create a mind map with the literary periods and their characteristic features to remind yourself of the connections.
Create practice questions: Create practice questions about the literary periods and try to answer them from memory. For example, "What characteristic features did the Romantic period have?"
Practice questions:

To which literary period do the works of Johann Wolfgang von Goethe and Friedrich Schiller belong?
What characteristic features did the Romantic period have?

When did the Enlightenment period take place and what characteristic features did it have?
To which literary period do the works of Marcel Reich-Ranicki and Günter Grass belong?
What characteristic features did the Modern period have and when did it take place?
Answers and elaboration:

The works of Johann Wolfgang von Goethe and Friedrich Schiller belong to the Classical literary period.

The Romantic period was characterized by emotionality, individual freedom, connection with nature, and interest in the past. It took place in the 18th and early 19th century.

The Enlightenment period took place in the 18th century and was characterized by rationality, belief in progress, and the desire to understand the world through reason and science.

5 Tips for incorporating Active Recall into your learning environment (Deep Work)

Set clear learning goals: Before starting to learn, you should set clear goals for what you want to achieve and in what time frame. For example, you could aim to complete a certain number of practice questions or read a specific chapter in a textbook within three hours.

Use the Pomodoro technique: Use the Pomodoro technique to focus on the current task while learning. This involves working for a set period of time (e.g. 25 minutes) with intense focus and then taking a short break (e.g. 5 minutes) afterwards. This way you can better focus on learning and not get distracted by external distractions.

Create a fixed study schedule: Create a fixed study schedule that includes time for Active Recall. Make sure to include enough breaks to rest and maintain concentration. This way you can avoid feeling overwhelmed or getting distracted by the hustle and bustle of the city.

Use quiet places for learning: Use quiet places for learning such as libraries, parks, or coffee shops in less crowded areas of the city. This way you can better focus on learning and not get distracted by noise and commotion.

Use headphones: Use headphones to shield yourself from external sounds and distractions. For example, you can listen to music or white noise to better focus on learning.

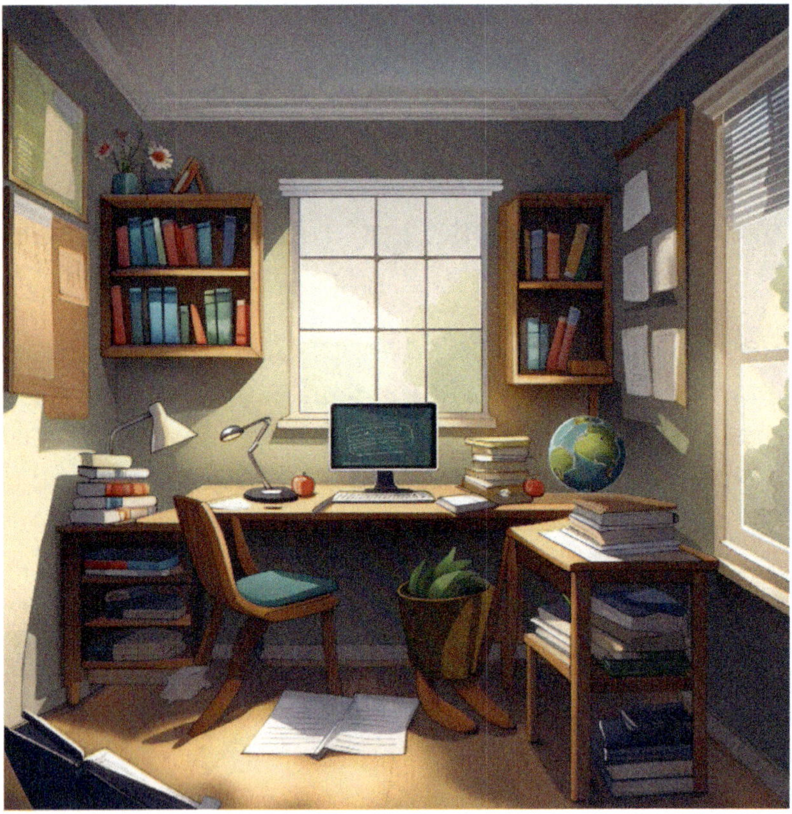

How can I set up my work environment to work effectively?

Create a fixed workspace: Find a fixed workspace for learning and design it to be comfortable and productive for you. This includes, for example, a comfortable chair, enough light, and good ventilation.

Reduce distractions: Make sure you have as few distractions as possible while learning. This includes, for example, turning off your phone and TV, avoiding noise, and avoiding unnecessary devices or objects in your work area.

Use visual aids: Use visual aids such as mind maps or timelines to better understand and retain what you have learned.

Create practice questions: Create practice questions on the topics that accompany your learning process.

Use post-it notes: Write your practice questions on small post-it notes and stick them on a wall or other visible place to remind you to practice.

Use Post-it notes: Write your practice questions on small Post-it notes and stick them on a wall or board in your work area. This way, you can take a quick break and work on a few questions without having to open your study materials. Create flashcards: Create flashcards with a practice question on one side and the answer on the other. You can hang them up in a convenient place in your work area and pull one out to study at any time.

Use Learning apps: Use learning apps that provide you with practice questions and help you deepen and solidify your knowledge. You can easily use these apps from your smartphone or tablet and work on a few questions at any time.

Quizlet: Quizlet is a learning app that provides you with flashcards with practice questions and answers. You can create your own flashcards or choose from existing sets. Quizlet also offers different learning modes, such as multiple-choice questions or listening to vocabulary.

Anki: Anki is a learning app that is based on the flashcard principle. You can create flashcards with practice questions and answers and then work on them. Anki also offers different learning modes, such as multiple-choice questions or listening to vocabulary.

Flashcards Deluxe: Flashcards Deluxe is a learning app that provides you with flashcards with practice questions and answers. You can create your own flashcards or choose from existing sets. Flashcards Deluxe also offers different learning modes, such as multiple-choice questions or listening to vocabulary.

Create practice sheets: Create practice sheets with practice questions and leave them in a convenient place in your work area.

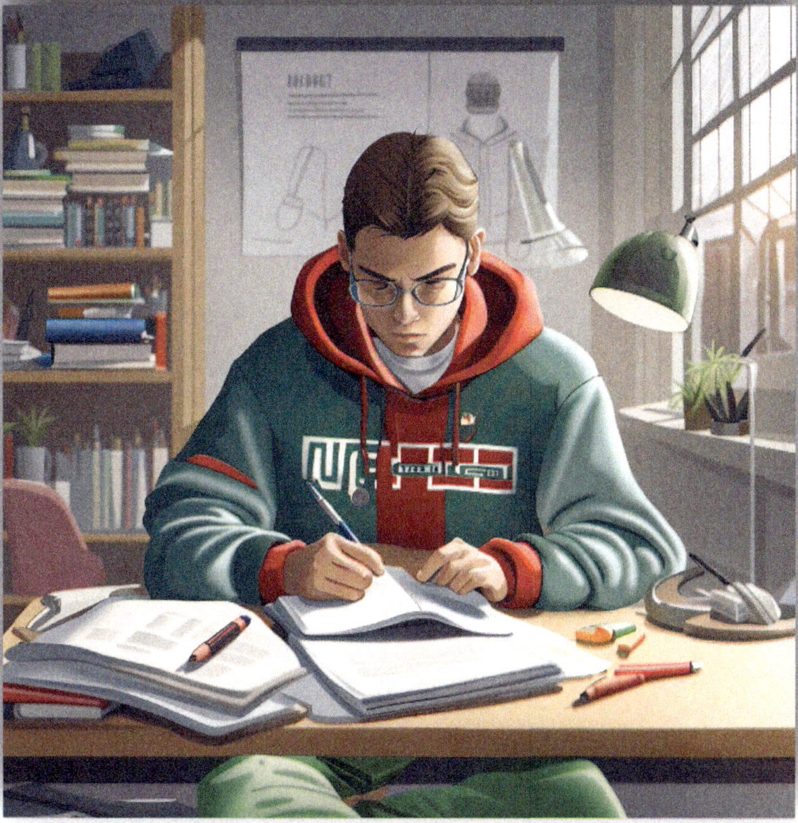

The power of flashcards in learning with Active Recall: How to improve your exam results and embed knowledge deeper in memory

Creating flashcards while learning can be a valuable method for students to learn with Active Recall and retain knowledge permanently. There are several reasons why flashcards can be helpful while learning: Flashcards allow information to be presented in a concentrated and clear way. Students can note the main points of a topic on a flashcard and therefore focus their attention on what is essential. Flashcards promote active thinking about what has been learned. Students must ask themselves questions while creating flashcards and try to recall the answers from memory. This embeds the information deeper in memory.

Flashcards support learning through repetition. Students can regularly review flashcards and recall the information again and again. Through regular repetition, the information stays in memory longer. Flashcards are mobile and can be taken anywhere. Students can, for example, learn flashcards on the subway or bus, making use of their learning time even when on the go. Flashcards can be customized to individual needs. Students can create their own flashcards and design them according to their personal needs and preferences.

Overall, flashcards in learning with the method of Active Recall offer many benefits and can be a valuable addition to other learning methods. It is worth trying flashcards as a learning method and seeing if they are suitable for one's own learning style. Some helpful tips can be found in the next chapters

Maximize your learning performance: With these 5 tips, you create effective flashcards

Use colors: Use colors to highlight important information and make your flashcard more visually appealing. For example, you can write the exercise question in a different color than the answer or highlight important information in a color that is particularly striking for you.
Use images and symbols: Use images and symbols to better understand and remember what you've learned. For example, you can draw a picture of a specific building or chemical symbol on your flashcard to better visualize what you've learned.

Structure your flashcard: Structure your flashcard by highlighting important information or presenting it in list form. This way you can better overview what you've learned and remember it more easily.

Use different font sizes and types: Use different font sizes and types to highlight important information and make your flashcard more visually appealing. For example, you can write the exercise question in a larger font than the answer or highlight important information in bold.

Color coding for flashcards

- Use colors that are significant to you: Use colors that are significant to you to highlight important information. For example, you can use red for important definitions, green for examples, and blue for possible exam questions.

- Use colors to highlight differences: Use colors to highlight differences, for example, to differentiate between different technical terms or concepts.

- Use colors to clarify the structure of the information: Use colors to clarify the structure of the information, for example, to differentiate between exercise questions and answers or to visualize the structure of a text.

- Use colors sparingly: Use colors sparingly and selectively to avoid overload and keep your flashcard clear. Don't use too many different colors and make sure the colors are readable.

Effective learning through color coding: Examples from the perspective of a German studies student

Use colors to mark different levels of analysis: For example, you could use red for the linguistic level, green for the content level and blue for the formal level. This way you can visualize the structure of your analysis and easily distinguish the different aspects from each other.

Use colors to mark different rhetorical devices: For example, you could use orange for hyperboles, yellow for metaphors and purple for rhetorical questions. This way you can easily identify the different devices in a text and analyze them more effectively.

Maximize your learning performance: With these 5 tips you create effective flashcards

Use colors: Use colors to highlight important information and make your flashcard more visually appealing. For example, you can write the exercise question in a different color than the answer or highlight important information in a color that is particularly striking for you.

Use images and symbols: Use images and symbols to better understand and retain what you have learned. For example, you can draw a picture of a specific building or a chemical symbol on your flashcard to better visualize what you have learned.

Structure your flashcard: Structure your flashcard by highlighting important information or presenting it in list form. This way you can better overview what you have learned and retain it more easily.

Use different font sizes and types: Use different font sizes and types to highlight important information and make your flashcard more visually appealing. For example, you can write the exercise question in a larger font than the answer or highlight important information in bold.

Color coding for flashcards:

- Use colors that are meaningful to you: Use colors that are meaningful to you to highlight important information. For example, you could use red for important definitions, green for examples, and blue for potential exam questions.
- Use colors to highlight differences: Use colors to highlight differences, for example, to distinguish different technical terms or concepts from each other.
- Use colors to clarify the structure of the information: Use colors to clarify the structure of the information, for example, to distinguish exercise questions from answers or to visualize the structure of a text.

- Use colors sparingly: Use colors sparingly and selectively to avoid overloading and keep your flashcard clear. Do not use too many different colors and make sure the colors are legible.

Maximize your exam success with summaries and Active Recall

As a student, one can use writing a summary as Active Recall by asking oneself questions about the read chapter of the book and trying to recall the answers from memory. By actively thinking about the content of the chapter, one can better understand and retain the most important information. One way to use writing a summary as Active Recall is to create questions about the most important topics of the chapter. For example, "What important insights are presented in the chapter?" or "How are these insights supported?" By answering these questions from memory, one can actively engage with the content of the chapter and understand it better. Another way to use writing a summary as Active

Recall by creating mind maps or diagrams that visualize the key information in a chapter. By organizing the information in this way, you will actively remember the content and be able to relate it to other information. Another way to use Active Recall while writing summaries is to create questions about the main topics of the chapter. This can be done before or after reading the chapter, for example, "What important concepts are discussed in this chapter?" or "What examples are given to illustrate these concepts?" By answering these questions, you will actively remember the most important information from the chapter and be able to summarize it.

Learning Anatomy with Active Recall: A Practical Guide for Medical Students

As a medical student preparing for the subject of Anatomy, it's important that you thoroughly read and understand the specific text on Anatomy. One way to process and retain what you've learned is by using Active Recall. A technique you can use while reading the text is making summaries.

By actively remembering what you've learned and summarizing the key information, you can better process the information and embed it deeper in your memory. For example, you could ask yourself questions like "Which structures belong to the upper extremity?" and try to infer the answer from the text. Or you could take note of the key points you want to retain from the text, to later review and deepen them. Another way to use Active Recall while reading the technical text is making mind maps or other graphical representations.

By visualizing the key information of the text and relating it to each other, you can better understand and more easily memorize the information. While reading the technical text, you could also try to apply what you've learned to other areas of anatomy. For example, you could ask yourself questions like:

"How are the structures of the cardiovascular system related to the skeleton of the body?" or "Which muscles are responsible for the movements of the hand?" By recognizing relationships and connections between different areas of anatomy, you can better understand and retain the information.

After reading the technical text, you could also move on to making summaries. By composing summaries, you can re-think the information and put it into your own words. You could also use Active Recall again by asking yourself questions and trying to retrieve the answers from memory. This way, you can actively engage with the information again and embed it deeper in your memory."

Learning 2.0: How the Leitner System and Active Recall Lead Students to Success

The Leitner System is a specific form of spaced repetition that helps to keep learned information permanently in memory. To use the Leitner System in combination with Active Recall, you can follow these steps:

Create flashcards with information you want to learn. On the front of the card should be a question or keyword, on the back the answer or explanation. Now ask yourself the questions on the flashcards and try to recall the answers from memory. If you know the answer correctly, put the card in a stack for "mastered" cards. If you don't know the answer, put the card in a stack for "not mastered" cards. After some time (for example, after a day or a week), repeat the process with all "not mastered" cards. If you answer a card correctly, put it in the stack for "mastered" cards. If you can't answer it again, put it in a stack for "difficultly mastered" cards.
Repeat the process with all "difficultly mastered" cards. If you answer a card correctly, put it in the stack for "mastered" cards. If you can't answer it again, put it in a stack for "very difficultly mastered" cards. Repeat the process until you have moved all cards to the stack for "mastered" cards. To keep the information permanently in memory, you should regularly repeat the Leitner System. For example, you can repeat all cards in the stack for "mastered" cards once a week, all cards in the stack for "difficultly mastered" cards every two weeks, and all cards in the stack for "very difficultly mastered" cards every four weeks. This way, the information remains in memory and does not have to be learned again from scratch."

A Step-by-Step Guide: How to Use the Leitner System as a Student with Active Recall

An example of how to use the Leitner System as a German literature student to learn the literary eras would be as follows: Create a list of the literary eras you want to learn, such as Middle Ages, Baroque, Enlightenment, etc. Create flashcards for each era with the most important information, such as important authors, characteristics of the era, significant works. Organize the flashcards using the Leitner System by sorting them into different compartments. Start with the "easy" compartment for flashcards that you already know well. Use the Leitner System by regularly quizzing yourself on flashcards from the "easy" compartment and then moving them to the "difficult" compartment if you answer incorrectly. Regularly review flashcards from the "difficult" compartment until you can answer them correctly, then move them to the "easy" compartment. Review flashcards from the "easy" compartment less frequently to solidify them in your memory. Regularly use the Leitner System to deepen and solidify your knowledge of literary eras.

Maximize your exam success with the powerful testing effect

The testing effect, also known as the "test king effect", describes the phenomenon that repeating learning material through testing or questioning the material is more effective than simply repeating it. This is because testing focuses the learner's attention more strongly, contributing to deeper encoding of the material in memory. For students, the testing effect offers a number of benefits: Improved memory performance: Testing learning material leads to deeper encoding of the material in memory and thus improved memory performance. Time saving: Testing learning material can help you acquire the material faster and more effectively, thus saving you time when learning. Exam success: The testing effect can help you better prepare for exams and thus achieve better results. Motivation: Testing learning material can help you feel more engaged and motivated when learning, as you can see quick progress and success. Overall, the testing effect in learning with Active Recall offers many benefits for students and can help you acquire the material faster and more effectively

Effective Learning in Legal Studies: The Testing Effect and Active Recall in Practice

The Testing Effect refers to the phenomenon that revisiting material through tests or quizzes can enhance learning progress and retention of information compared to mere reading or listening. The Active Recall approach focuses on the active engagement with material by generating questions and answering them, which also contributes to improved learning progress.

To leverage the Testing Effect, a first-semester law student could consider the following strategies:
Creating quizzes or tests after each study segment: The student could formulate questions for themselves or search online for quizzes to review and solidify their learning.
Conducting study groups with tests or quizzes: Teaming up with fellow students to mutually pose questions and conduct quizzes can boost motivation and foster a sense of competition.

Enhancing lecture or seminar slides with questions or tasks: The student could take notes and formulate questions related to the covered content to deepen understanding and reinforce learning.

Enrolling in exam preparation: Various courses and resources tailored for legal exam preparation often include tests and quizzes to assess learning progress. Registering for such preparation can further harness the Testing Effect.

Maximizing Learning through Active Recall: How to Efficiently Manage Time and Energy

As a student in a bustling metropolis, your plate is full, and finding ample time and energy for studying can be challenging. However, with the right approach, you can effectively harness Active Recall for learning and make the most of your time and energy.

Active Recall, as demonstrated earlier in this book, involves repeatedly retrieving learned information to train your memory and enhance content retention. It's not just about repeating the material; it's also about quizzing and processing it in various forms. This approach ingrains the content more deeply in your memory and facilitates easier retrieval.

Tips for Efficient Time and Energy Management while Practicing Active Recall Learning

Utilize your time effectively: Plan your study sessions in advance and make use of time slots when you're particularly focused and motivated. Choosing the right study environment can also contribute to effective time utilization.

Prioritize tasks: Consider which content holds greater significance for your studies and concentrate on that. This way, you avoid getting lost in insignificant details.

Maximize Your Learning Potential: How Spaced Repetition and Active Recall Collaborate to Optimize Your Memory

The concept of Spaced Repetition is a technique used to internalize and retain information through repeated learning. It's based on the idea that the brain retains information better when it's revisited at regular intervals. To successfully leverage Spaced Repetition for your learning, there are several steps you can follow:

Carefully select the content to learn: Utilize materials that are relevant and interesting to you.
Break down the content into small, manageable learning segments: This makes learning easier and less overwhelming.

Set realistic learning goals: Determine how much time you can allocate for studying and how much you intend to learn in each session.

Use various learning methods: Experiment with different techniques to internalize the material, such as creating mind maps or writing summaries.
Employ tools to organize and track learning: There are numerous tools available to help you plan and monitor your learning, such as flashcards or learning apps.

Repeat the learned material at defined intervals: Schedule regular review sessions to solidify your learning. For instance, you can decide to review specific content the next day, after a week, and after a month.

Regularly take tests: By testing yourself on the learned material, you can ascertain whether you've truly internalized the content.

Stress-Free Learning: The Key to Sustainable Learning Success with Active Recall

Providing a general recommendation for time allocation when using Spaced Repetition for students preparing for an exam with a one-month timeline is challenging, as it depends on various factors such as the exam's difficulty level, the student's prior knowledge, and the scope of the material to be learned.

However, a good starting point could involve revisiting the learned material at regular intervals while employing longer time spans to reinforce learning. For instance, you might attempt to review the study material every three days and gradually increase the time intervals as your exam date approaches. Another approach could be breaking down the content into smaller sections and revisiting them at regular intervals.

It's crucial to tailor your time allocation to your individual needs and take the time to discover which time intervals work best for you. Regular testing is also beneficial to assess how well you've retained the material. This way, you can address weaknesses effectively and prepare for the exam in a targeted manner.

3 Tips for Adjusting Time Intervals in Learning

Here are 3 tips on how you can properly set time intervals for studying for an exam as a student: Consider the exam's difficulty level and prior knowledge: Determine the time intervals based on the exam's difficulty level and your prior knowledge. If the exam is more challenging and you have less prior knowledge, shorter time intervals might be more effective.

Start with longer intervals and gradually reduce them: To reinforce learning, it could be beneficial to initially use longer time intervals and gradually shorten them as the exam date approaches. Customize time intervals individually: Take your learning style and personal preferences into account when setting time intervals. Experiment with different time spans and adjust them based on how well you're retaining the material.

It's important to tailor time intervals to your individual needs and take the time to discover which intervals work best for you. This way, you can prepare for the exam strategically and effectively internalize the learned material.

Harnessing the Power of Study Groups: 3 Tips for Applying Active Recall

Here are three examples of how Active Recall can be effectively implemented in a group setting through flashcards:

Flashcard Creation Competition: Divide the group into teams and challenge them to create as many flashcards as possible on a specific topic within a set timeframe. Participants must actively utilize their knowledge and ask each other questions to ensure the flashcards are accurate and comprehensive. Flashcard Bingo: Divide the group into teams and assign each team a set of flashcards with different terms or concepts. The teams then aim to figure out the terms or concepts on their flashcards by asking questions to other teams or through collaborative discussions.

Flashcard Quiz: Divide the group into teams and provide each team with a set of flashcards containing various terms or concepts. The teams then attempt to explain the terms or concepts on their flashcards by asking questions to other teams or through collaborative discussions. The other teams must then try to guess the explanations and provide the correct answers.

These are just a few examples of how Active Recall can be applied in a group setting through flashcards. There are many other possibilities, such as creating quiz games or discussing case studies. It's essential for participants to be actively engaged and apply their knowledge actively to deepen and reinforce their learning.

The SMART Method: The Key to Consistent Excellence as a Student

Here are some tips to consider while studying as a student to stay motivated and consistently achieve high performance: Set Realistic Goals: It's crucial to establish achievable goals to avoid feeling overwhelmed and demotivated. Goals should be specific, measurable, attainable, relevant, and time-bound (SMART goals).

Create a Study Plan: A study plan helps structure learning material and track progress. You can set daily, weekly, or monthly targets and allocate time slots for working on each goal.

Utilize Active Recall: Active Recall is a learning method where you actively retrieve information from memory rather than passively reviewing it. This can be done through quiz questions, discussions with others, or creating summaries.

Reward Yourself: To maintain motivation, consider rewarding yourself for reaching milestones. These rewards could be small treats like a tasty snack or a brief walk.

Seek Support: Getting assistance from others while studying can be beneficial, whether it's from peers or a tutor. Participating in study groups or engaging with friends and family can also help boost motivation.

It's essential to remember that everyone learns and gets motivated differently. Therefore, it's advisable to experiment with various techniques to figure out what works best for you.

Successful Studying with SMART Goals: A Guide for (Medical) Students

A medical student can set SMART goals by considering the following criteria:
Specific: The goal should be clearly defined and specific. Example: "By the end of the semester, I want to understand and confidently apply all learning materials from the Anatomy module."

Measurable: The goal should be measurable, allowing you to track progress and reflect on your achievements later. Example: "By the end of the semester, I aim to comprehend and confidently apply at least 75% of the Anatomy module's learning materials, which I will assess through regular tests and quiz questions."

Achievable: The goal should be realistic and attainable, preventing you from feeling overwhelmed and demotivated. Example: "I will allocate a minimum of 10 hours per week to study the Anatomy module and establish a dedicated study space and time to achieve this goal."

Relevant: The goal should be personally relevant and significant to the medical student, aligning with their interests and objectives. Example: "I want to excel in the Anatomy module because I aspire to be a proficient physician in the future, necessitating a strong grasp of anatomy to provide excellent patient care."

Time-Bound: The goal should have a specific timeframe for achievement to provide a clear deadline and facilitate progress tracking. Example: "By the end of the semester (in 3 months), my goal is to thoroughly understand and confidently apply all learning materials from the Anatomy module."

Successful Studying with SMART Goals: A Guide for (German Studies) Students

A student studying German Studies, particularly with a focus on teaching, can set SMART goals by considering the following criteria: Specific: The goal should be clearly defined and specific. Example: "By the end of the semester, I want to develop and successfully implement at least 3 different teaching introductions for math lessons."Measurable: The goal should be measurable, allowing you to track progress and reflect on your achievements later. Example: "By the end of the semester, I aim to develop and successfully implement at least one teaching introduction for math lessons, for which I will seek feedback from my teaching mentor and students."Achievable: The goal should be realistic and attainable, preventing you from feeling overwhelmed and demotivated. Example: "I will allocate a minimum of 2 hours per week to creating teaching introductions for math lessons and establish a dedicated study space and time to achieve this goal."

Relevant: The goal should be personally relevant and significant to the student, aligning with their interests and objectives. Example: "I want to develop teaching introductions for math lessons because I aspire to motivate and inspire my future students as a teacher, requiring engaging introductions."

Time-Bound: The goal should have a specific timeframe for achievement to provide a clear deadline and facilitate progress tracking.

Example: "By the end of the semester (in 3 months), my goal is to develop and successfully implement at least 3 different teaching introductions for math lessons in my practical teaching experience."

Challenges and Solutions in Learning through Active Recall and How to Deal with Them

Active Recall can enhance memory retention and retrieval during learning. However, there are also challenges and issues that can arise when using Active Recall:

Time Commitment: Active Recall can be time-consuming, as it demands more effort than passive review of study material. Hence, allocating sufficient time for learning and setting realistic expectations is vital.

Overwhelm: Active Recall might lead to feelings of overwhelm, especially if the material isn't fully understood or the questions are too difficult. In such cases, it can be helpful to revise the material again or seek support from others.

Motivation: Active Recall might become monotonous and less motivating when repeatedly recalling the same information. To maintain motivation, try varying learning methods, rewarding yourself, or sharing your learning journey with others.

Mistakes: Mistakes can occur during Active Recall, leading to incorrect memorization or confusion. It's important to accept mistakes as part of the learning process and use them to deepen understanding and retention.

"The biggest mistake you could ever make is to be afraid to make mistakes." - Dale Carnegie

Example of Potential Challenges: A student wants to memorize the names and key features of the planets in our solar system using Active Recall. They create quiz questions and attempt to recall the answers from memory. During the process, they find it time-consuming and occasionally overwhelming. They try motivating themselves with small rewards and seek assistance from others when unsure. Despite encountering errors, they use these mistakes as opportunities to better remember and comprehend the planets.

3 Mistakes a (Medical) Student Could Make While Learning Active Recall and How to Avoid Them

A medical student aiming to memorize the functions of the heart using Active Recall might make various mistakes while learning, for instance:

Overloading: The student might attempt to memorize too many heart functions at once, leading to feeling overwhelmed.

Insufficient Understanding: The student might try memorizing the heart functions without adequately comprehending the underlying knowledge. This could result in incorrect or mixed-up memorization.
Lack of Variation: The student might repeatedly tackle the same heart functions, lacking variety in their learning, potentially leading to boredom or demotivation.

In Active Recall, where information is repeatedly retrieved, a medical student could make the following mistakes while memorizing heart functions: They might try to memorize all the information at once instead of breaking it into smaller units. This could overwhelm the student and hinder effective memorization.

They might not connect the information in a contextual framework, treating it merely as a series of facts. This can make recalling the information more difficult, as it lacks a broader context.
They might not engage in regular repetition of the information, instead opting for a single learning session and hoping it sticks in memory. However, memory retention improves through repeated exposure.

They might let distractions, such as prolonged TV watching or other activities, interfere with their learning. This reduces study time and impairs information retention.

To avoid these mistakes, the student could employ the following strategies:
Learn information in smaller segments and regularly review them.

Memorize information within a contextual framework by understanding examples and real-world applications.

Allocate consistent time for learning while avoiding distractions.

Utilize learning techniques like flashcards or the Leitner system to train memory and enhance information retention.

Active Recall for Students - A Summary

Active Recall is an effective method for enhancing learning and improving knowledge retention. It involves regularly recalling learned content from memory to enhance understanding and retention. Compared to passive learning, where content is merely listened to or observed without active engagement, Active Recall is a far more efficient method for retaining knowledge.

Setting clear and specific learning goals is a crucial prerequisite for learning with Active Recall. These goals should be SMART, meaning they should be specific, measurable, achievable, relevant, and time-bound. This allows for progress tracking and self-motivation.

Various review methods can be employed while learning through Active Recall, including summarization, question answering, mind mapping, and discussions. Using diverse review methods is essential to make learning more effective.
Allocating enough time for review is another key aspect of learning with Active Recall. Regularly revisiting the learned material is crucial for improved understanding and retention. Focusing on the most important content and discerning between vital details and less crucial ones is also vital.
To summarize, here are the top 10 ideas for students using Active Recall:

Set clear and specific learning goals: Make these goals SMART – specific, measurable, achievable, relevant, and time-bound.

Use various review methods: Summarization, question answering, mind mapping, and discussions are some examples.

Allocate enough time for review: Regular revision is vital for enhanced understanding and retention.
Focus on the most important content: Distinguish between essential and non-essential details.
Set realistic goals: Avoid overwhelming yourself and set attainable objectives.

Vary your review methods: Employing different review techniques enhances learning effectiveness.
Minimize interruptions: Try to stay as focused as possible during Active Recall sessions.
Utilize visual aids: Visualizations and diagrams can enhance understanding.

Work in short study intervals: Short intervals aid concentration.

Reward yourself for progress: Remember to acknowledge and reward your achievements to maintain motivation.

It's important to note that Active Recall might not suit all subjects, and there are alternative learning strategies that might be more suitable for certain situations. Experimenting with various strategies is important to find what works best for you and your learning goals. With the right approach, Active Recall can be a potent method for improving learning and retaining learned content effectively.

Bibliography

1. "The Science of Active Learning" von R. Karpicke und J. Roediger

2. "Incorporating Active Learning into College Courses" von J.M. Prince

3. "Make It Stick: The Science of Successful Learning" von P.C. Brown, H.L. Roediger III und M.A. McDaniel

4. "Active Learning: A Practical Guide" von J.B. Prince

5. "The Power of Active Recall: Revolutionize Your Learning with Spaced Repetition" von A.M. Owen

6. "Metacognition, Strategy Use, and Instruction" von J. Flavell

7. "Promoting Deep Learning through Effective Pedagogy" von D. Boud und N. Molloy

8. "The Role of Practice and Feedback in the Acquisition of Declarative and Procedural

9. Knowledge" von R.K. Sweller und J. Sweller

10. "The Role of Spacing in Long-Term Retention" von J.R. Anderson und J.D. Neely

11. "A Review of Research on the Benefits of Spaced Practice" von K.A. Rawson and J.M. Dunlosky.

Notes for KEYLEARNINGS